GROUNDBREAKERS

Louis Pasteur

Ann Fullick

Heinemann
LIBRARY

www.heinemann.co.uk
Visit our website to find out more information about **Heinemann Library** books.

To order:
 Phone 44 (0) 1865 888066
 Send a fax to 44 (0) 1865 314091
 Visit the Heinemann Bookshop at www.heinemann.co.uk to browse our catalogue and order online.

First published in Great Britain by Heinemann Library,
Halley Court, Jordan Hill, Oxford OX2 8EJ
a division of Reed Educational and Professional Publishing Ltd.
Heinemann is a registered trademark of Reed Educational & Professional Publishing Ltd.

OXFORD MELBOURNE AUCKLAND
JOHANNESBURG BLANTYRE GABORONE
IBADAN PORTSMOUTH (NH) USA CHICAGO

Designed by AMR
Illustrated by Art Construction
Originated by Ambassador Litho Ltd
Printed in Hong Kong/China

ISBN 0 431 10441 7 (hardback)   ISBN 0 431 10453 0 (paperback)
05 04 03 02 01   05 04 03 02 01
10 9 8 7 6 5 4 3 2   10 9 8 7 6 5 4 3 2 1

British Library Cataloguing in Publication Data
Fullick, Ann
  Louis Pasteur. – (Groundbreakers)
  1.Pasteur, Louis – Juvenile literature
  2.Chemists – France – Biography – Juvenile literature
  3.Vaccines – History – Juvenile literature
  I.Title
  540.9'2

Acknowledgements
The Publishers would like to thank the following for permission to reproduce photographs:
AKG photo: pp10, 26; Bridgeman Art Library: p4; J Allan Cash: pp17, 28; Collections: Sandra Lousada p43; Corbis: pp5, 27; Mary Evans Picture Library: pp8, 19, 30, 34, 37; Hulton Getty: p11; Oxford Scientific Film: p18; Institut Pasteur Musée: pp6, 7, 9, 14, 15, 24, 25, 32, 33, 35, 36; Science Photo Library: pp12, 16, 20, 31, 40, 41; Still Pictures: p39; Trip: H Rogers p38; Wellcome Library: p42.

Cover photograph reproduced with permission of Science Photo Library.

Every effort has been made to contact copyright holders of any material reproduced in this book. Any omissions will be rectified in subsequent printings if notice is given to the Publisher.

Any words appearing in the text in bold, **like this**, are explained in the glossary.

Contents

Turbulent times

France in the early 19th century was a country in turmoil. The Napoleonic wars were over and people were picking up the threads of their lives, but the legacy of the **French Revolution** – when so many great thinkers and scientists had been sent to their deaths at the **guillotine** – still hung over the country. On 27 December 1822 Louis Pasteur was born into these turbulent times.

A hard life

In those days most jobs were done by hand, and most people lived lives of constant physical labour. There was also little or no defence against disease. Almost every family saw children die young, mothers die from infection following childbirth, or fathers die from infected work injuries.

Because no one understood the cause of these diseases, no one could cure them. Louis Pasteur carried out an amazing amount of scientific work during his lifetime, but perhaps most important was his work on **infectious diseases**. By the end of his life he had explained how infectious diseases were spread and made **vaccination** against some of them possible.

In the early days of the 19th century life was hard for everyone, but it was hardest of all for the poor. These Breton farmers are digging up potatoes.

*Louis Pasteur – his lifetime of work ranged from the chemistry of **crystals** to the germ theory of disease, and included vaccination against infectious diseases such as anthrax and rabies.*

A day to remember

On 15 October 1831, when Louis was just 8 years old, a rabid wolf made its way down from the mountains and went berserk, attacking people at random. Eight of the victims later developed rabies and died. Several people in Louis' village were bitten, and they all went to the blacksmith for the only known treatment for rabies – to have the wounds cauterized or branded with red-hot iron. The young Louis Pasteur heard their dreadful screams, saw their terror and smelt the burning flesh – in years to come these images remained with him and drove him on with his research.

A great legacy

The legacy of Louis Pasteur is truly a great one. His lasting achievements include exciting new discoveries in chemistry; developing methods of preserving wine and milk; saving the silkworm industry; and finally producing explanations and cures for infectious diseases, including rabies.

The Pasteur family

Louis drew this portrait of his mother, Jeanne, when he was 13. The drawings he did as a schoolboy were of an amazingly high standard – none of his other school work was as good.

The Pasteur family

The Pasteur family came from humble origins. For centuries they had worked in the fields as agricultural workers and then as tenant farmers. Gradually they had moved to become tradesmen, and Louis Pasteur's father, grandfather and great-grandfather were all **leather tanners**.

Monsieur and Madame Pasteur

Louis' father, Jean-Joseph Pasteur, was drafted into the French army when he was 20, and served with such distinction that he was awarded several medals. Jean-Joseph was proud to be part of a victorious French army under Napoleon, and regarded these as his 'glory days' for the rest of his life.

When Jean-Joseph returned to civilian life in Salins near the Swiss border, and took up his old trade of tanning, life must have seemed very dull compared to his adventures at war. However, before long he began courting a local gardener's daughter, Jeanne Etiennette Roqui, and in 1816 they were married. They soon moved to the nearby town of Dôle and it was here that they started their family before moving again to Arbois.

Brothers and sisters

Their first child was a son, but the joy following his birth soon turned to sadness when he died in infancy. Jeanne's second baby, born in 1818, was a daughter, and then four years later Jean-Joseph and Jeanne welcomed their third child – another boy – into the world. He was born on 27 December 1822 and they named him Louis – Louis Pasteur, a name which was to become famous the world over. The family was completed with the birth of two more daughters, so Louis grew up in Arbois as the only boy among a brood of girls.

Growing up

Louis seems to have had a fairly happy childhood, brought up to be loyal to the family, to work hard and take good care of money. His father hoped that he might one day become a teacher in the local school, leaving behind the messy, smelly world of tanning, and this seemed a possibility.

By the time Louis drew this portrait of his father he was 15, and the standard of his other school work had improved. It was becoming obvious that he was destined to work with his brain and not just his hands.

Louis was a good but not outstanding pupil at the local school, a hard worker who showed no real talent except for drawing!

Gaining an education

Louis did not shine during his early years in school, but as he got older his intellect began to develop. In 1837, when he was 15, he won almost all of the school prizes. He now set his sights on the most prestigious colleges in Paris to continue his education and study to become a teacher.

The search for success

Louis decided to aim for a place at the Ecole Normale, and went to study at a specialist boarding school in Paris. However, he was so dreadfully homesick and unhappy that after a month he returned home and went back to his old school.

Three months before his 18th birthday, Louis gained his **baccalauréat**. His marks for every subject were 'good' except for elementary science – these were 'very good'. This made Louis determined to study science, so he worked for two more years to gain his baccalauréat in science. When he finally achieved this his mark in physics was 'passable' and in chemistry 'mediocre', so his undoubted genius was still not evident!

A pupil at the Ecole Normale in 1848. Louis Pasteur had to work very hard to achieve a good result in the entrance exams for the Ecole Normale, the best teacher training institute in France at that time.

Louis was finally offered a place at the Ecole Normale, but his marks were among the lowest that year. Not satisfied, he turned down the offer and went back to the school he had previously left out of homesickness. This time he stayed, and gradually his hard work and diligence began to be matched by his achievements. When he finally took up his place at the Ecole Normale he was fourth on the list of candidates in the science section.

The scientist emerges

Between the years of 1843 (when he was 21) and 1848, Louis Pasteur worked away at the Ecole Normale. He studied hard, did a certain amount of teaching and took up a number of research projects. In 1847 he was made a doctor of science and quickly made his mark in the scientific world.

Louis blossomed during his time as a student, and by the age of 24 he was beginning to have ideas that would feed his research for many years to come.

Pleasing his father with a teaching career in some small French town no longer appealed to Louis – he now set his sights on a high-flying scientific career among the greatest scientists in Paris. But in 1848 revolution rocked the city of Paris, and the plans of Louis Pasteur, like those of so many others, were thrown into turmoil.

Revolution

The French National Guard at the palace of Versailles. Louis joined the National Guard in 1848, a municipal **militia** with the job of maintaining civil order. He also gave all of his savings – 150 francs – to the republic.

The first **French Revolution**, which changed the entire history of the nation and affected all of Europe, had taken place in 1789. At the beginning of this later French revolution, in February 1848, Louis Pasteur, along with many others, simply tried to keep out of the way. However, when the Second Republic was declared in April, it became impossible to remain on the sidelines any longer and Louis joined the National Guard.

A personal loss

Reports of the fighting and difficulties in Paris spread like wildfire to the provinces. Back in Arbois, Louis' family – particularly his mother – worried about him a great deal. Paris and their only son seemed a long way away. At the end of May 1848, Jeanne Pasteur was suddenly taken ill and died of what appeared to be a burst blood vessel in the brain. Louis was grief-stricken and blamed himself for the anxiety he had caused, which he was sure had contributed to his mother's death.

Louis' father was now living alone with the responsibility for Louis' three sisters, all unmarried and in their 20s, one of whom was severely retarded as a result of a dreadful childhood fever. In spite of the fact that it meant leaving Paris and all of his research, Louis asked to be transferred to a more provincial post relatively close to his remaining family.

Life moves on

Louis was appointed professor of physics in Dijon in September, but did not take up his appointment until December, as he had some crucial research to finish in Paris before he moved. In spite of his concerns immediately after his mother's death, Louis did not stay close to his family for long – ambition drove him on. He had only been in Dijon a few weeks when he successfully applied for, and won, the post of acting professor of chemistry at the **Faculty** of Sciences at Strasbourg. He took up his post in January 1849.

In Pasteur's words:

In writing to his prospective father-in-law Louis explained his family background and their modest financial situation. He also made clear that he felt any money left by his father should go to support his three sisters. All Louis was offering was *'good health, a good nature, and my position in the University.'*

A whirlwind romance

Arriving in Strasbourg towards the end of January 1849, Louis immediately met Marie Laurent, the daughter of the rector of the Strasbourg Academy. By 10 February he was writing a formal letter of proposal to her father, asking permission to marry his daughter!

Louis obviously made a good impression on all concerned because on 29 May 1849, when he was 26 years old, he and Marie were married. During the early years of his marriage he settled into a period of very productive work, which was to bring him wide-ranging recognition.

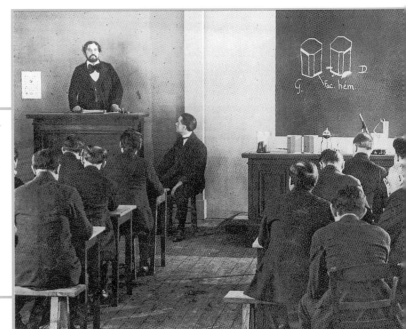

Louis Pasteur lecturing at the Faculty of Sciences, Strasbourg. Although Louis threw himself into his teaching and research when he took up his post in Strasbourg, he also put a lot of effort into his personal life as he courted Marie Laurent.

Crystallography

When the young Louis Pasteur was searching for topics on which to base the research for his doctorate at the Ecole Normale in Paris, he became influenced by Auguste Laurent. As a result Louis began work on the **molecules** of water held within the **crystal** structures of various chemicals.

Solving the paratartrate riddle

Louis became skilled in the use of **polarized light** in the study of crystals. Normal light is made up of a mixture of light rays travelling in random directions, but in a beam of polarized light the rays are travelling in the same direction.

The German chemist Mitscherlich had found two chemicals which he thought were identical. These were sodium-ammonium **tartrate** and sodium-ammonium paratartrate.

Crystals have different shapes and different numbers of faces depending on which chemical they are made of. These copper sulphate crystals are sparkling as light reflects off their faces.

However, he was puzzled to find that while the tartrate rotated polarized light to the right (it was **optically active**), the paratartrate appeared to have no effect at all on polarized light. Pasteur's work solved this problem and provided a major breakthrough in the understanding of crystal structure.

By very careful observation of the paratartrate crystals, Pasteur found that some of the crystals were right-handed and bent polarized light to the right. Others were left-handed crystals and bent light to the left. When mixed together in the normal compound these cancelled each other out and made it look as if the substance was optically inactive. Finally he showed that solutions of the two compounds had exactly the same effect on polarized light as the crystals themselves. This meant that the effect on polarized light was due to differences in the molecules themselves – and it was these differences which affected the way the crystals formed.

Legend has it that in April 1848, when Louis made his discovery, he rushed out of his laboratory and hugged a curator of the university whom he found in the corridor! True or not, the story reflects Pasteur's excitement at his discovery.

There were personal excitements too. In 1850 Louis and Marie celebrated the birth of their first child, a daughter called Jeanne, and in 1851 their only son, Jean-Baptiste, was born. Over the next few years they added three more daughters to their family.

AUGUSTE LAURENT

Louis' first mentor was Auguste Laurent (1807–1853) – a brilliant scientist, but with radical ideas and a difficult personality. Louis gained much from his advice on crystals, but as Laurent fell from favour in the scientific community with the arrival of new ideas, Pasteur quickly moved his loyalties to Gabriel Delafosse and Jean-Baptiste Biot. These two were also experts in crystallography, and were much more socially and scientifically acceptable.

Pasteur was not just a good scientist – he knew that it mattered who you were associated with, and by 1860 he had removed all reference to Laurent from his lectures. By the time Laurent died at the early age of 46, almost forgotten by the scientific community, Louis Pasteur's star was well on the rise.

Louis Pasteur in 1857, aged 34, while dean of the Faculty of Sciences at Lille.

On 2 December 1854 Louis Pasteur was officially appointed professor of chemistry and dean of the new **Faculty** of Sciences at the University of Lille in northern France. Part of the job of this new faculty was to use science to support and help the thriving local industries. Lille was then in the heartland of mining and industrial France. Louis took this aspect of his job description to heart, and it was a close association with local manufacturers which was to launch him on the next stage of his research career.

Pasteur the organizer

In his new position Louis had to concentrate on the administration of the faculty as well as on his research. He quickly showed that this was another of his many talents, and soon introduced laboratory-based teaching for all the science subjects. Before this, science students had been given lectures and watched some demonstrations but had not worked in laboratories themselves. Learning science in this way must have been fairly dull and distant.

Louis also worked very hard at forging links between local industry and the faculty. He took students on trips to factories in Belgium, to look at the techniques they used to produce and purify metals. He also got them testing manures to be used in agriculture. He ran courses teaching the science behind some of the more important local industries – bleaching, sugar-making and refining, and most particularly the **fermentation** and refining of the local speciality, beet **alcohol**.

Beet and Monsieur Bigo

One of the big businesses in the area around Lille was the use of beet to make sugar, or the fermentation of sugar to produce alcohol. Louis Pasteur became increasingly interested in the process of fermentation, although the reasons for this interest have never been entirely clear.

The story goes that one of Louis' pupils, Monsieur Bigo, was the son of a local beet alcohol producer. When his father and others suffered a really difficult year, with fermentations which went wrong and produced little or no alcohol, Bigo asked his illustrious teacher for advice. Louis certainly made frequent visits to the factory, and demonstrated that a healthy fermentation showed round yeast globules under a microscope, but if the fermentation went wrong then long rod shapes could be seen.

Pasteur's private laboratory notes have only been made public relatively recently. They reveal that he was driven at least as much by his own scientific interest, as by a desire to help the local community – although in the end his work has been of huge benefit to people all around the world.

However, it seems that the truth is probably less flattering to Pasteur. From his own notes it seems he had been interested in the process of fermentation for some time, not to help his local community, but because some of the alcohols which could be produced did not seem to fit in with his theories on **crystal** shapes.

Fermentation

In 1857 Louis Pasteur decided to change the whole thrust of his research. He left behind his obsession with the details of **asymmetrical molecules** and **crystals**, and moved on to something with far wider appeal – **fermentation** and why fermenting liquids are **optically active**. His work was to have far-reaching effects on the brewing of beer and the production of wine right up to the present day.

In the meantime his wife Marie worked hard behind the scenes, acting as his secretary, listening to his ideas and bringing up their children.

A new way of seeing

Fermentation had long been regarded as a process of disintegration – the sugar that people knew was needed for the formation of alcoholic drinks broke down, and one of the products of this breakdown was **alcohol**. Pasteur knew this could not be right. Sugar is optically active, but once it is broken down the activity goes. So where was the optical activity he measured in alcohols coming from? Pasteur knew that only living organisms are capable of creating new, asymmetrical molecules and so, he reasoned, fermentation itself must be a living process.

A yeast cell magnified many times. Pasteur showed that fermentation is brought about by living yeast cells such as these – a breakthrough for the makers of beer and wine.

Fermentations on the scale of this massive brewery would simply not be possible if Louis Pasteur had not found out about the tiny micro-organisms which make it happen, and the conditions they like to work in.

Louis showed that fermentation produces not just carbon dioxide and ethanol, but also other chemicals such as succinic acid. He emphasized the complexity of fermentation, and used this to confirm his ideas that the reactions must be linked to a living organism. He went on to prove this experimentally. If yeast is mixed with pure sugar solution and ammonium nitrate, then ethanol is formed. If any of the ingredients are removed then no fermentation takes place.

ONGOING IMPACT) Wines and beers

When Louis Pasteur showed that fermentation is a process brought about by a living organism it had enormous implications for the brewing industry and wine producers. Living organisms need carefully controlled conditions. They function best if their waste products are removed regularly, and the temperature at which they work is crucial. Pasteur's discovery has made it possible for brewing and wine-making to change from small-scale, local industries to large, factory-based operations, with millions of litres fermented every week.

Spontaneous generation

For centuries people had believed in **spontaneous generation** – the idea that living things come into being spontaneously by the will of God. But by Louis Pasteur's time some people were beginning to doubt the idea. This doubt led to other problems, as it implied a lack of belief in the power of God. There was no clear evidence either way. Someone needed to conclude the debate – and this is what Pasteur set out to do.

Félix-Archimède Pouchet (1800–1872) was a man of 60, a respected naturalist from Rouen in north-west France, when he came into conflict with the 37-year-old Louis Pasteur over spontaneous generation. Pouchet had had a long career in traditional biology, specializing in the development of embryos and reproductive biology. He was director of the Natural History Museum in Rouen and a member of the **Académie des Sciences** in Paris.

Did moulds spontaneously appear on food and frogs emerge from mud by the will of God, as people believed, or from cells and organisms that were already there? Louis Pasteur was determined to find out.

After a long and distinguished career, Pouchet had decided that under certain circumstances fertilized eggs arose spontaneously and then developed into adult organisms. In 1858 he published a paper in which he claimed to prove that this type of spontaneous generation had occurred in an experiment he had carried out. He claimed that micro-organisms had appeared in boiled hay infusions which he had stored under mercury after exposing them to oxygen. In 1859 he then produced an enormous book on the theory of spontaneous generation in which he brought together all the evidence he could find to support his theory. He brought in experimental evidence, evidence from embryo development and theological and religious views, claiming they all showed he was right.

Félix-Archimède Pouchet was a well-respected member of the scientific community and certainly no light-weight opponent for Pasteur!

Pasteur's initial response to Pouchet was very quiet, for he had done very little work on spontaneous generation himself. However the work that he had done suggested that micro-organisms only appeared in such a broth if air was allowed to enter. Thus Louis thought that the micro-organisms which appeared in Pouchet's broth had almost certainly already been present in air which had accidentally been admitted to the experiment. He wrote an almost apologetic letter to Pouchet suggesting that this might be the explanation – but within a year this polite exchange of ideas had been replaced by a furious and rather bitter quarrel.

The swan-necked flasks

Louis Pasteur became determined to show that ordinary air contained living organisms – and that it did not possess some 'mysterious principle' which caused **spontaneous generation** when conditions were right.

At the same time he and Marie were coping with the loss of their eldest child Jeanne. She died of typhoid fever, one of the many **infectious diseases** rife at the time. The death of 9-year-old Jeanne hit Louis hard, but he still pressed on with his work.

The proof of the pudding

Pasteur showed that if he pumped atmospheric air through a plug of cotton wool, it became full of microscopic living organisms. Pasteur believed it was these organisms that started to grow when air got into any sealed vessel. He went on to set up three elegant experiments to prove once and for all that spontaneous generation did not occur.

Firstly Louis cleverly tried Pouchet's own method and found that even in his own expert hands the method gave very inconsistent results – one up to Pasteur!

Secondly he boiled up a sugar and yeast mixture in a flask, killed the yeast to show nothing could grow, filled the flask with **sterile** air and then sealed it in a hot flame. Nothing grew in it for six weeks – then Pasteur introduced one of his wads of cotton wool loaded with microbes from the air and sealed the flask again. Within 36 hours the liquid in the flask was teeming with familiar micro-organisms.

Pasteur believed – rightly – that micro-organisms like these were the source of the life that developed in the sealed flasks.

Pasteur suggested that the growth in the fluid must come from the microbes in the air. He knew that some of his opponents would still be unconvinced – he could imagine them arguing that life had spontaneously generated from the organic material in the cotton wool – so he repeated the experiment using a mineral material (asbestos), and got exactly the same results.

The swan-necked flasks

Now Pasteur felt he had proved that nothing was needed for microbial life beyond the germs found in the air itself – it was the beginning of his germ theory. He published his papers on 8 February 1860. By May he had extended his work to growths on milk and urine. Pouchet's ideas were finished and **pasteurization** was just around the corner.

In 1863 Marie gave birth to their fifth child, a baby daughter whom they called Camille.

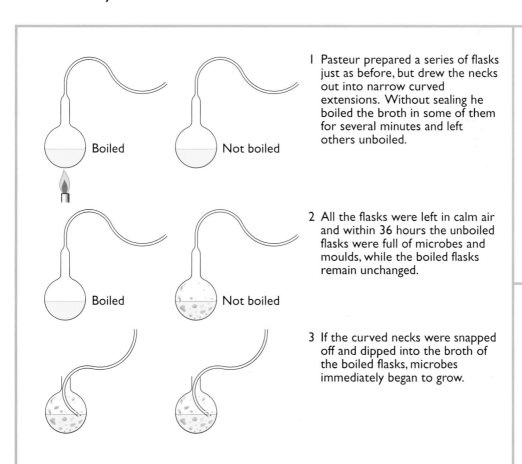

Boiled   Not boiled

1 Pasteur prepared a series of flasks just as before, but drew the necks out into narrow curved extensions. Without sealing he boiled the broth in some of them for several minutes and left others unboiled.

Boiled   Not boiled

2 All the flasks were left in calm air and within 36 hours the unboiled flasks were full of microbes and moulds, while the boiled flasks remain unchanged.

3 If the curved necks were snapped off and dipped into the broth of the boiled flasks, microbes immediately began to grow.

From the elegant simplicity of these experiments Louis Pasteur concluded that the 'swan necks' trapped germs from the air, preventing them from reaching the broth and growing.

The silkworm crisis

In the 18th and 19th centuries France had a flourishing silkworm industry worth 10 million francs a year. No wonder the mulberry – the tree on whose leaves the silkworm feeds – was known as 'the tree of gold'! But by the early 1860s a mysterious disease was destroying the silkworms and the silk industry was falling apart.

The problem

The disease **pébrine** attacked silkworms at any stage of the lifecycle. The main symptom was little black or brown spots appearing, followed rapidly by the death of the silkworm or moth. The disease first appeared in 1845 and by 1846 it was rampant in France, Italy, Spain, Austria – even China was attacked. Eventually Japan was the only remaining disease-free country and healthy silkworm eggs

The silkworm is not a worm at all – it is the caterpillar of the silk moth. It turned out to be vulnerable to the new and deadly disease pébrine in every stage of its life cycle.

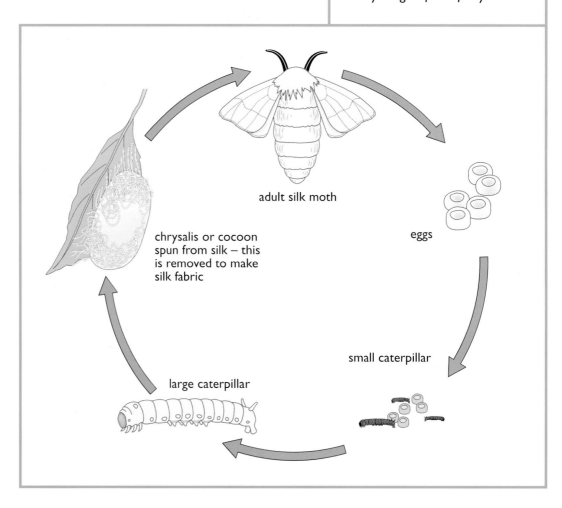

adult silk moth

eggs

chrysalis or cocoon spun from silk – this is removed to make silk fabric

small caterpillar

large caterpillar

had to be bought from there. The livelihood of thousands of people was being destroyed and poverty, starvation and disease followed close behind.

In desperation J. B. Dumas, a French government senator, wrote appealing to Louis Pasteur to come to the aid of this, one of France's most important industries. Pasteur had solved the problems of the brewing industries and the wine-makers. Could he now act as saviour to the silkworms?

The solution

In June 1865 Louis Pasteur arrived in Alais (now called Ales) to begin his research, having read everything he could about silkworms. It involved waiting months for moths to develop before the results of each investigation were made fully clear. Yet within three years of travelling between Alais and his home in Paris, he had devised a way by which growers could be sure that their eggs – and therefore the caterpillars which would hatch out of them – were clear of disease.

Pasteur did all this immensely valuable work at a time of great personal sadness. In June 1865 his beloved father died and in September his youngest daughter, 2-year-old Camille died too. Camille's death came after weeks of fever. Louis and Marie had sat up night after night nursing their child, and her death left Louis exhausted and bereft.

In Pasteur's words:

Louis was very concerned at the request from Dumas, and not at all sure that he had the expertise to help. He wrote:

'Your proposition … is indeed most flattering and the object is a high one, but it troubles and embarrasses me! Remember, if you please, that I have never even touched a silkworm. If I had some of your knowledge of the subject I should not hesitate …'

In Pasteur's words:

To his great sorrow Louis was not with his father when he died. He wrote a touching and affectionate letter to his wife and children from Alais to tell them what had happened.

'For thirty years I have been his constant care, I owe everything to him. When I was young he kept me from bad company and instilled into me the habit of working … How glad I am that he saw you all again a short time ago, and that he lived to know little Camille.'

The man himself

Louis and Marie Pasteur – she supported his work throughout their marriage and was described by one fellow scientist as 'his greatest collaborator'.

Louis Pasteur was always grateful to his parents for the support they gave him as he grew up, and for their ability to accept and encourage his desire for learning. His mother died when he was still a young man, but his father lived to realize that through Louis the name of Pasteur would be remembered for a very long time.

The family man

Louis was not a particularly attentive husband – his work was too absorbing for that – and Marie accepted this, acting as his help-mate, partner and secretary. On their 35th wedding anniversary she wrote to their surviving daughter, Marie-Louise: 'Your father, very busy as always, says little to me!' In spite of this, Louis' marriage to Marie was long and successful, lasting 45 years in total.

Their son Jean-Baptiste never had any children, which disappointed Louis who would have liked to see the family name continue. It fell to his youngest and only surviving daughter, Marie-Louise, born in 1858, to produce the longed-for grandson. She married René Vallery-Radot, a popular writer who would later produce a masterly biography of his father-in-law, and they named their son Louis Pasteur Vallery-Radot.

But this is leaping forward into the future. In the late 1860s Pasteur was a well-established scientist, respected by many but known and liked by rather fewer. Some people were put off by his stern manner and dedication to work, yet he was loyal and supportive of those he deemed worthy of his friendship. He was tremendously organized and fastidiously clean. His understanding of the role of invisible micro-organisms in causing disease may have been behind his frequent washing not only of his hands, but of his eating and drinking utensils as well!

Struck down in his prime

On 19 October 1868, when Louis Pasteur was 45 years old and achieving great things, disaster struck. He suffered a severe stroke which left him paralyzed down his left side and with his speech badly affected. He was given the best of available treatments – bleeding with sixteen leeches, electric shocks – and nursed devotedly by Marie. As a result he recovered sufficiently to take up once again the threads of his life and work – but his speech, walking and ability to use his hands were affected for the rest of his life. His great mind was unaffected, but in future the ideas and experiments Pasteur dreamed up would have to be carried out mainly by the hands of others.

Louis and Marie had five children whom they adored. Louis was remarkably active in their care for a man of his generation, and it was a cause of great distress to him that Jeanne, Camille and finally Cécile died as children. This picture shows Louis and Marie in 1892 with their only son Jean-Baptiste, their daughter Marie-Louise, her husband and their grandchildren.

The battle against infection

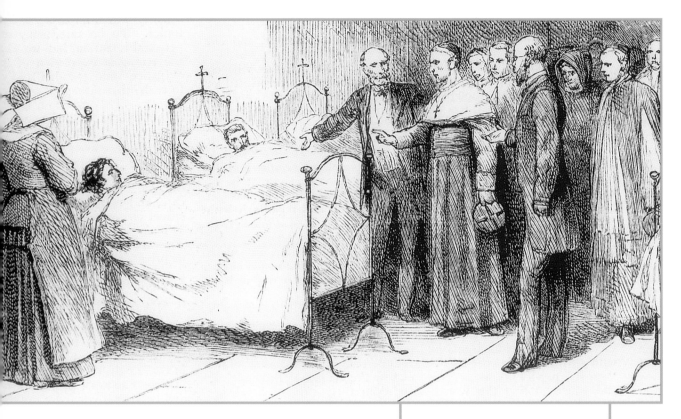

When Louis Pasteur announced his intention to move the focus of his research to the study of **infectious diseases**, the delighted French government granted him the money to build and equip a new laboratory to use for this very purpose.

A cholera ward in a 19th-century hospital. Thousands of men, women and children died of infectious diseases at this time. Pasteur's own three little daughters were among them.

Building in Paris started just at the time when Pasteur was struck down by his stroke and, as he was expected to die, work ground to a halt! Pasteur could see and hear the building site from his home, and as he began to recover he found the lack of progress on his new laboratory deeply distressing. When Emperor Napoleon III heard of this he wrote personally to ensure that building work started again immediately. Greatly enthused, Pasteur returned to work – against his doctor's advice – only three months after his stroke. The great new laboratory was completed in 1871, but Pasteur did not actually begin his work on infectious diseases until 1877.

The curse of infection

It is hard for us, at the start of a new millennium, to realize the terrible scourge of infection in the 19th century. There were no **antibiotics** to turn back the course of an infection. Surgery was very dangerous because the almost inevitable infection of the wound meant operations usually resulted in death. In maternity hospitals, almost a quarter of women died from infection in the first few days after giving birth. It was this helplessness and suffering which made Pasteur determined to find out the cause of these infections and prevent them.

JOSEPH LISTER

Joseph Lister (1827–1912) was a British surgeon who read Pasteur's germ theory of **fermentation** and made the mental leap that it might be similar 'germs' which cause infection. He developed the use of **carbolic acid** to kill those germs and so prevent infection during and after surgery. In Lister's wards all of the surgical instruments and dressings were sterilized in carbolic solution before use. The surgeons and their assistants washed their hands in carbolic solution before operating or changing dressings. In the operating theatre a fine spray of carbolic was used to create an **antiseptic** atmosphere. In 1874 Lister wrote to Pasteur, telling him of his progress and expressing gratitude for the way in which Pasteur's work had helped him in his thinking.

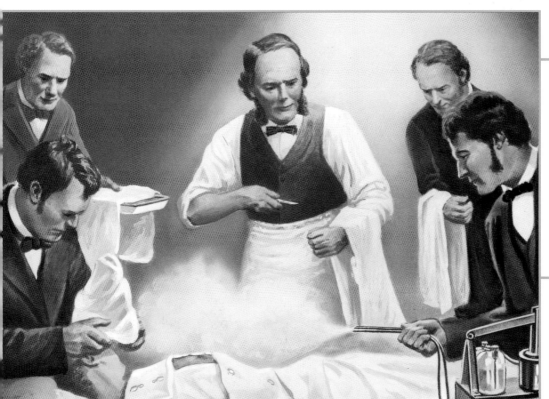

Lister introduced the revolutionary idea of sterile operating theatres and hospitals, and the survival rates of patients soared.

The battle over anthrax

Anthrax is caused by the bacterium *Bacillus anthracis*. The blood of the affected animal becomes packed with bacteria, large, swollen, blistering pustules form on the body and **septicaemia** sets in. It is almost always fatal and can attack humans as well as farm animals, entering through broken skin. Most frighteningly, anthrax **spores** survive in the soil for many years.

The search for a vaccine

Between 10 and 50 per cent of French flocks of sheep and herds of cattle were being lost to charbon or splenic fever (as anthrax was known) each year. Pasteur and his team were confident of producing a **vaccine** for anthrax but it was not as easy as they hoped. The bacterium proved difficult to grow at first, and then seemed impossible to make safe.

Pasteur tried all sorts of treatments – heat, chemicals such as potassium bichromate and oxygen – yet none seemed to give reliable results. To add to the pressure, Jean-Joseph Henri Toussaint, a young vet, claimed to have produced a successful

The Scottish island of Gruinard, in the distance, was infected with anthrax spores during World War II as part of an exercise in germ warfare. It remained uninhabitable for over 40 years.

vaccine by heating anthrax-infected blood to 55 °C for 10 minutes. Pasteur discovered that vaccine produced in this way was very unreliable, and in February 1881 announced that he too had developed a new anthrax vaccine. Because he was such a well-known figure people took notice of Pasteur's vaccine.

Scientific development on Pasteur's vaccine was then interrupted by a very public challenge to demonstrate its effectiveness. This was issued by Hippolyte Rossignol, a veterinary surgeon who had little or no time for Pasteur's germ theory. Rather than look unsure of his science, Pasteur accepted the challenge, though he was not certain that his vaccine would work!

ROBERT KOCH

In 1876 Robert Koch, a young German doctor, decided to join the debate on anthrax and its cause. He developed a medium in which he could grow the bacterium, and found that using **aqueous humour** from the eye made their growth amazingly rapid. He also observed the formation of spores, and when he infected guinea-pigs, mice and rabbits with his culture they all developed anthrax and died.

The trial at Pouilly-Fort

1 On 5 and 17 May 25 sheep were given Pasteur's anthrax vaccine.
    25 similar sheep were given no vaccine.
2 On 31 May all 50 sheep were injected with virulent anthrax spores. Pasteur predicted that the vaccinated sheep would survive.
3 On 2 June press, scientists and the public gathered at Pouilly-Fort to see the results.
    The vaccinated sheep were all alive.
    The unvaccinated sheep were mostly dead, some were dying of anthrax.

After the triumph of Pouilly-Fort, Pasteur completed the development of his vaccine which had a major effect on farming for generations to come. At home too he was enjoying the fruits of family life. His son Jean-Baptiste was married and had become a diplomat, and his daughter Marie-Louise was engaged to marry the writer René Vallery-Radot.

Rabies

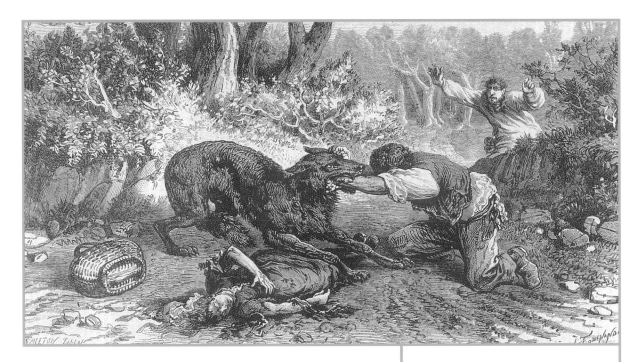

In Louis Pasteur's time rabies was – as today – very rare in people. Yet rabies struck fear into the bravest heart. The **incubation period** lasts months or even years after the bite of a rabid animal, and once the symptoms started to show there was no hope – death was the only way out.

Rabies is also known as hydrophobia, or fear of water. Eventually sufferers cannot even bear to swallow their own saliva. This picture from a 19th-century French magazine shows a rabid dog attacking a group of people.

The sheer horror of the disease is made clear in an account, written in 1795, of the death of a young English weaver (page 31). Even today, without **vaccination**, the course of rabies is still dreadful. There are pools of infection in wild animals in many parts of the world, including Europe and the USA, but not the UK.

Pasteur's choice

As a boy Louis Pasteur had been deeply affected by the attack of a rabid wolf on his own village, and now as an eminent scientist he decided he must turn his attention to rabies. There were no more than 100 human cases of rabies a year in France, but rabid animals were relatively common, and the disease so dramatic that Pasteur could not resist attempting to find a **vaccine**. He knew that if he was successful, not only would great fame and glory be his, but it would also prove his germ theory once and for all to those who were still sceptical.

The rabies microbe

Pasteur wanted desperately to find the microbe that was causing rabies, and searched for it in the saliva, blood and brains of infected animals. He never found it, yet Pasteur was sure a microbe was causing the disease and that he would be able to culture (grow) it, weaken its intensity and produce a vaccine.

In May 1795 a weaver named John Lindsay arrived at a hospital in Manchester, England. He was terrified that he might have rabies, as a result of a rabid dog bite many years previously. When asked to drink a little cold water he could scarcely get any down, and he was frightened by any noise or person approaching. Over the next couple of days doctors were distressed to see the way he struggled to swallow food or liquid.

John was frantic to prove he did not have rabies because he had a wife and six young children to support; but despite his determination the disease took hold. He began to twitch and spasm at the slightest sound or touch. He had difficulty breathing and severe pain in his stomach and chest. He could not swallow his saliva and began to spit constantly. John had terrifying hallucinations, yet he could still answer questions quite sensibly. After three days his racing heart began to falter. Finally the poor man had a massive convulsion and died.

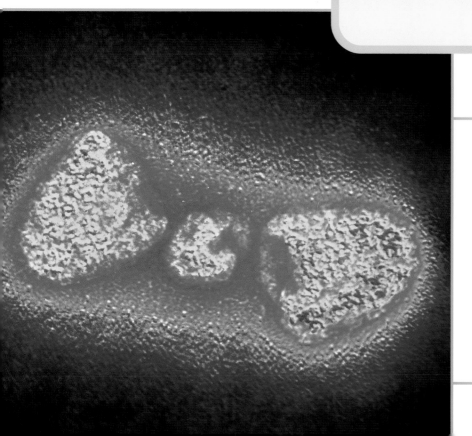

The rabies virus is so small it would have passed through every filter, and been invisible to even the most powerful microscope available when Pasteur was working. Today the modern technology of the electron microscope allows us to see it.

31

Success !

Pasteur dipped in and out of his work on rabies, but time and time again he returned. With Pasteur hot on the trail, it was only a matter of time before the problem of rabies was solved.

One of the biggest problems facing research into rabies was that in dogs, symptoms only developed a month or more after infection. Pierre-Victor Galtier, a veterinary surgeon of Lyon, discovered that rabies could be transmitted to rabbits, almost halving the **incubation period** to 18 days. Galtier also had other ideas which Pasteur picked up and secretly worked on, until in 1884 he went public with some amazing news – he had discovered a way of producing weakened **vaccines** which could make dogs **immune** to rabies itself.

Then all went quiet again until …

Human guinea-pigs

On Monday 6 July 1885 three terrified visitors arrived at Louis Pasteur's laboratory. Two of them had been bitten by a rabid dog two days earlier. The dog's owner was safe as his skin had not been punctured, but little Joseph Meister, comforted by his frantic mother, was in a bad way. Two separate doctors agreed that the child faced certain death from rabies. So, with the family's permission, Pasteur set out to treat him with a technique which had so far only been tried on dogs.

Young Joseph Meister was bitten by a rabid dog more than a dozen times on his hands, thighs and calves. The bites were so deep he could hardly walk. Yet Pasteur's experimental vaccine saved his life.

Over eleven days he was given thirteen injections of the rabies virus, each more virulent than the last. After this the boy went home – and never developed rabies. Pasteur was jubilant, but told no one except his wife Marie and their two remaining children, who, although they were both married, remained closely in touch with their father and his work.

Three months later Pasteur was contacted about a 15-year-old shepherd, Jean-Baptiste Jupille. When he and other shepherds had been attacked by a rabid dog, Jean-Baptiste saved the younger boys by fighting and killing the dog – but he was severely bitten himself. Was there anything Monsieur Pasteur could do to help save this brave and selfless young man?

Pasteur was Jean-Baptiste's only chance – and it worked. The gruelling series of injections gave him immunity from the disease and he returned home cured. The prevention of rabies was the final major discovery of Pasteur's long and distinguished career – and it ensured him a place in the history books.

Pasteur immediately agreed to treat local hero Jean-Baptiste Jupille, but warned that as the treatment would be starting several days after the bite, the chances of success were lower than when Joseph Meister was treated. To his delight the young man survived.

The man and the myth

Louis Pasteur was a great man and a great scientist – of that there is no doubt. But there are two sides to everyone, and as Pasteur's private notebooks have become public, some of his doubts and hesitations have become known. While most scientists welcomed a free exchange of ideas, he was a very secretive worker. He would work for a long time before publishing any results, partly, it seems, to prevent fellow scientists using his work.

The Pasteurians

This secrecy was made possible by the dedication of Pasteur's wife Marie – who throughout their marriage acted as his confidante – and by the group of loyal workers Pasteur built up around himself, who became know as the 'Pasteurians'. This group, which included Dr Emile Roux, worked to support Pasteur and carry out the tasks he could not manage himself. They left it to the 'Master' to decide when the results should be made public.

On the other hand Pasteur himself was always ready to use the ideas of other scientists to help him overcome a particular problem. While in some cases he acknowledged the help he received, there were times when he simply used other people's results without any acknowledgement.

Researchers who worked with Pasteur were expected to show fierce loyalty both to the man and his ideas. Whenever queries about Pasteur's ethics or methods were raised, his supporters could simply answer – look at his results!

Pasteur at work in his laboratory in 1885. In his private laboratory notebooks he confided many misgivings and concerns.

Hidden doubts

Pasteur's public image was of a supremely confident man who never allowed any uncertainty to show. Everyone knew about his successes in treating the boys bitten by rabid dogs. However, the release of his private laboratory notebooks in 1964 showed that Pasteur had earlier treated two other people bitten by rabid dogs.

In 1885 he briefly treated a 61-year-old man who probably never had rabies, and a 6-year-old girl, Julie-Antoinette Poughon, who had been bitten on the lip by her own puppy which had become rabid. She received two injections of Pasteur's **vaccine**, but died of rabies within a day. These two were never mentioned publicly by Pasteur. Only two weeks after the death of little Julie-Antoinette he tried out a new method – successfully – on Joseph Meister.

A strong man

Unlike many scientists, Louis Pasteur was very politically aware. He knew who to influence and how to ensure that he and his family were well provided for financially. Louis would discuss his work passionately with his wife and children, revealing his insecurities and concerns, but he never allowed any such 'weaknesses' to be made public. After suffering a debilitating stroke while still in his prime, he drove himself on to make some of the most influential scientific and medical discoveries of the 19th century.

One of Pasteur's flasks containing the dried spinal cord of a rabbit which had died of rabies. Pasteur was convinced that his new method of preparing a rabies vaccine – using dried spinal cords – would prove effective, even though it wasn't properly tested before he tried it.

The end of the story

The French government recognized the immense implications of Pasteur's work on germ theory and **vaccination**, and invested heavily in a superb research complex in which he could carry on his work. This great building was to be known as l'Institut Pasteur (the Pasteur Institute). It was completed in 1888, but in 1887 Pasteur suffered a further series of small strokes and was never again well enough to work in his own laboratories.

Louis took great comfort from his only grandson in his old age.

The overseer

Pasteur's failing health did not cloud his mind. Although he could no longer work actively himself, he could oversee and supervise the group of other researchers and students (the 'Pasteurians') who were following in his footsteps. They took it upon themselves to carry on the work of the 'Master', and began to tackle yet another of the dreaded **infectious diseases** of the time. **Diphtheria** killed thousands of children every year, and the workers at the Pasteur Institute set themselves up to produce a **vaccine** against it.

By this stage Pasteur was becoming increasingly frail. He was receiving honours from all over the world as countries across the globe benefited from the work he had done. There was no **Nobel prize** for science or medicine in Pasteur's day – but if there had been, he would surely have received it at least once if not twice. When he turned 70 he was presented with a medal inscribed: 'To Pasteur, on his 70th birthday. France and Humanity grateful' – and that summed up the worldwide recognition of his work.

Death

The infirmities of age began to close in on Louis Pasteur. In 1894 he suffered another stroke, and by his death he was almost completely paralyzed. When his final illness set in he was nursed night and day by a combination of his family and his work colleagues. Marie, his devoted wife, spent most of her time at his bedside and his beloved grandchildren came in each day to cuddle him and chat. In spite of all their care, Louis Pasteur died aged 72, at 4.40 in the afternoon on Saturday 28 September 1895.

A nation mourns

The death of Louis Pasteur affected the whole French nation, for he had brought great honour and fame to his country and had benefited the whole human race.

After a period of lying in state in the Pasteur Institute, Pasteur was given a massive state funeral on 5 October 1895, after which his body was returned to an ornate mausoleum in the institute which bore his name. The whole country mourned the death of a man who, in his life's work, had saved the lives of so many others in France and around the world.

After his death, the body of Louis Pasteur lay in state in an ornate room in the Pasteur Institute.

Pasteur's legacy

Pasteurized milk has had an enormous impact on the health of people in many countries. In particular it has reduced the spread of diseases such as TB.

Louis Pasteur lived and worked in the 19th century, a time when many modern ideas about science and medicine were only just beginning to emerge. In one way or another, his legacy touches us all.

In the euphoria which surrounded Pasteur's later work it is easy to forget his early success in the field of **tartrates** and **isomers**. Pasteur's discovery of isomers which rotate **polarized light** in different directions has had far-reaching implications both in materials science (the science of matter) and in biochemistry. There is now a branch of science known as **stereochemistry** which studies the arrangement of **atoms** and **molecules** in space. The **optical activity** of substances is an important aspect of this discipline, and it all began with Louis Pasteur.

Good wine, good beer, safe milk

Across the world the brewing industry and wine growers have an enormous impact both on people's social lives and on the economies of nations. By unfolding the secrets of the processes which send wine and beer sour, Pasteur made possible the enormous expansion of these industries, which can now produce large quantities of reliable products. Milk which is safe to drink is another massive legacy of Pasteur. **Pasteurizing** milk kills off most of the harmful bacteria it contains, which means we can drink it without the risk of catching diseases like tuberculosis (TB). The milk also lasts longer before going off.

TB is a disease caused by bacteria, which particularly attacks the lungs. It was a major killer in Pasteur's time, and in many countries is still a relatively common cause of death.

The battle against disease

It is in the battle against the devastation of **infectious disease** that the work of Louis Pasteur has had its greatest effect. It was largely due to Pasteur that the idea that diseases are spread by germs (microbes) became accepted by scientists, doctors and the public alike. This key realization alone, which seems so obvious now, has saved millions of lives. People now understand the importance of hygiene in everyday life, and the risk of infection between a sick and a healthy individual.

However, it was perhaps Pasteur's work on **vaccination** which has had the most dramatic legacy. Many of the most virulent and dangerous infectious diseases, in people and domestic animals, are now controlled by vaccination.

A baby in Zimbabwe receives a vaccination. The life expectancy of young children in the developed world, and increasingly in the developing world, has been greatly increased by vaccinations against the most common childhood diseases.

Whilst experimenting in the 1860s, Pasteur realized that the microbes which caused milk to go off, and **fermentations** to fail, could be killed by heat, and that liquids treated in this way would last for much longer. Heat treating milk, beer and other liquids to preserve them soon became common practice, and the process was known as 'pasteurization' in honour of Pasteur.

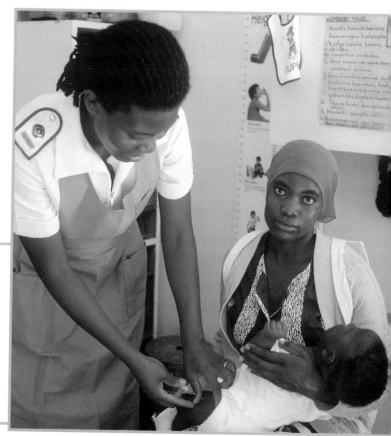

L'Institut Pasteur

Another crucial aspect of the legacy of Louis Pasteur is the institute of scientific research which bears his name. Founded in 1887 by Pasteur himself, l'Institut Pasteur is a private, non-profit making organization. It was originally set up in Paris as a centre for the treatment of rabies, a research centre for **infectious diseases** and a teaching centre. It is still all of these things.

Pasteur was not only committed to basic research but also to its practical applications. Those who have followed after him have maintained this tradition, from Emile Roux and Alexandre Yersin, who both worked with Pasteur himself, to the scientists working with the Institute today.

Some great scientists ...

Many famous scientists have worked at the Pasteur Institute. Roux and Yersin discovered a treatment for **diphtheria**, a major killer, particularly of children. Many **Nobel prize** winners have also emerged from the Institute:

- Elie Metchnikoff in 1908 for contributions to the understanding of the **immune** system which fights disease in the body
- Jules Bordet in 1919 for discoveries about immunity to diseases
- Charles Nicolle in 1928 for his work on the way that typhus is transmitted, a problem which had been a complete mystery for many years
- Jacob, Monod and Lwoff in 1965 for shedding light on the regulation of viruses.

More than a century after the death of Louis Pasteur, scientific research goes on, both at the original Pasteur Institute in Paris shown here, and at other branches of the Institute set up in the USA and around the world.

... and great science

Much of modern preventative medicine has its origins in the Pasteur Institute. **Vaccinations** against diphtheria, tuberculosis, tetanus, yellow fever, polio and **hepatitis B** were all developed there, along with the use of anti-bacterial drugs for treating bacterial infections. Since World War II the Institute has focused on **molecular** biology. In recent years scientists at the Institute have discovered HIV, the virus responsible for **AIDS**, as well as the bacterium responsible for causing many stomach ulcers. They have produced a **genetically engineered vaccine** against hepatitis B and developed tests for the early detection of colon cancer and *Helicobacter pylori*.

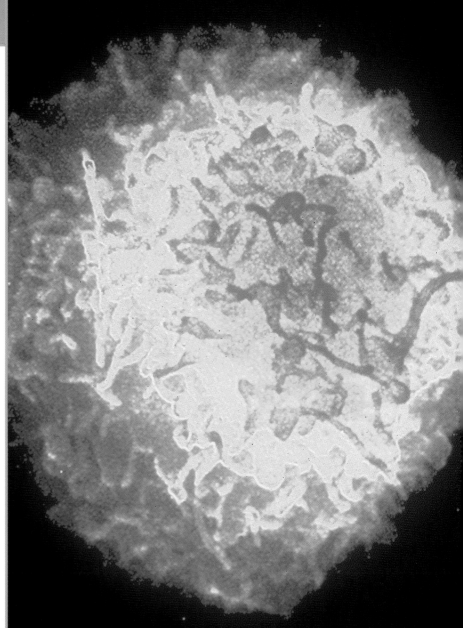

A blood cell infected with HIV. The discovery in the 1980s of the virus which causes the dreadful new disease AIDS has been one of the Pasteur Institute's more recent triumphs.

The Pasteur Institute in Paris now houses 100 research units, with hundreds of scientists from 70 countries working there. It runs a teaching hospital and is at the centre of a global network of 24 Pasteur Institutes. It forms a fitting memorial to a remarkable man.

A giant among giants

The work of Louis Pasteur has had an enormous impact on human lives and the way in which society has developed since he first made his remarkable discoveries.

When Pasteur began his scientific work as a young man, a lot of the accepted explanations for disease had not been challenged for many, many years. People believed that life was spontaneously created by God wherever moulds or other organisms seemed suddenly to appear. By the time Pasteur died, as we have seen, much of the old belief had been stood on its head and a more modern, scientific view of the world was accepted by experts and the public alike.

The list of his achievements is long – **stereochemistry**, beer and wine production, **pasteurization**, germ theory, **vaccination**, the defeat of rabies – and it continues to grow, through the research done in his name at the Pasteur Institutes throughout the world.

A tribute to Pasteur entitled: 'A Benefactor of Humanity'. Not many scientists receive this type of homage when they die!

Current research includes the study of cancer and the search for **vaccines** against many diseases including **AIDS** and several tropical diseases such as **malaria**, **dengue** and the *Shigella bacterium*. The expertise of the 'Pasteurians' in just this type of work leads to hope that they will soon find some answers.

A scientist of genius

Louis Pasteur was a man whose scientific work was of such immense value to his fellow people that he achieved greatness and appreciation during his own lifetime, not just among the scientific community but also among ordinary people. They might not have understood exactly what Pasteur was doing, but they certainly recognized that they and their children were more likely to live because of it.

That sense of greatness has not diminished with time. We still recognize that in Louis Pasteur we were visited by one of the truly great scientists. His influence will continue on into the new century just as it has filled the last, because his discoveries and his visions were ones that will not fade.

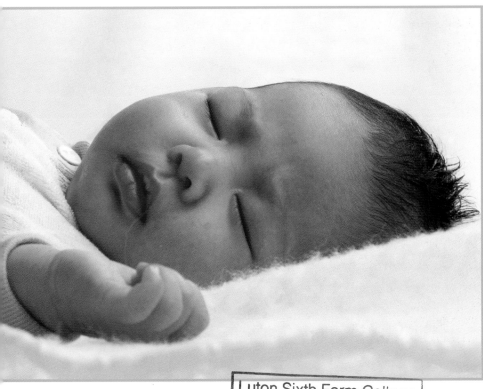

Babies and their parents can sleep more peacefully in the knowledge that through the work of Louis Pasteur – on hygiene in hospital wards, on pasteurizing milk, and on vaccination against serious diseases – a baby born today stands a good chance of growing into a healthy adult.

Timeline

1789	The **French Revolution** begins.
1815	Napoleon is defeated.
1816	Louis' parents, Jean-Joseph Pasteur and Jeanne Etiennette Roqui are married.
1822	Louis Pasteur is born on 27 December in Dôle, in France.
1831	On 15 October a rabid wolf attacks people in Louis' home village of Arbois; eight people later die of rabies.
1831–39	Louis is a student at the College d'Arbois; he gains his **baccalauréat**.
1842–43	Student at Barbets School and Lycée St-Louis, Paris.
1843–46	Studies at the Ecole Normale, Paris; he also teaches there.
1847	Becomes a doctor of science and begins to study **crystals** and the **optical activity** of **tartrates**.
1848	Paris is rocked by revolution, and the Second Republic is declared. Jeanne Pasteur, Louis' mother, dies.
1849	Louis moves to Strasbourg University as professor of chemistry; on 29 May he marries Marie Laurent.
1850	Louis and Marie's first child is born, a daughter called Jeanne; over the next few years they have four more children, three of whom die in childhood.
1854–57	Louis is professor of chemistry and dean of the **Faculty** of Sciences, University of Lille.
1857	Louis begins to study **fermentation** and **spontaneous generation**.
1863	Marie gives birth to their fifth child, a daughter called Camille.
1865	Louis' father Jean-Joseph and his youngest daughter Camille both die.
1865–68	Louis studies the silkworm disease **pébrine**.
1867–88	Director of the laboratory of physiological chemistry, Ecole Normale.
1868	Louis suffers a severe stroke which leaves him paralyzed down his left side; despite this he continues to work, with the help of his assistants, the 'Pasteurians'.
1871	The French government builds a new laboratory for Louis in Paris, in which he later studies **infectious diseases**.

1874	Joseph Lister develops the theory that germs cause infection from Pasteur's work, and introduces the use of **carbolic acid** as an **antiseptic** in operating theatres.
1877	Louis begins to study the causes and prevention of infectious diseases, including anthrax and rabies, in his new laboratory.
1885	Louis successfully treats two boys who have been infected with rabies.
1887	Louis founds the Pasteur Institute in Paris, as a centre for the study of rabies and other infectious diseases.
1888–95	Louis is director of the Pasteur Institute, Paris.
1895	On 28 September Louis Pasteur dies, aged 72.

Places to visit and further reading

Places to visit

The Pasteur Institute Museum in Paris, France

The Pasteur Institute website at web.pasteur.fr which has information about Pasteur himself and about past and current work

The Science Museum, London, UK – particularly the display of the Wellcome Wing on the history of medicine. You can visit the museum on the internet at www.nmsi.ac.uk

Further reading

Shuter, Jane: *Health and Medicine* – A Century of Change series (Heinemann Library, Oxford, 1999)

Tames, Richard: *Penicillin* – Turning Points in History series (Heinemann Library, Oxford, 2000)

Thomson, Pat: *The Silkworm Mystery: The Story of Louis Pasteur* – Super Scientists series (Hodder Wayland, London, 1998)

Wallace, Karen: *Louis Pasteur* (Franklin Watts, London, 1997)

Glossary

Académie des Sciences Science Academy

AIDS Acquired Immune Deficiency Syndrome – a disease which causes the breakdown of the human immune system and so leaves the body open to attack by infectious diseases

alcohol common name for the chemical ethanol, C_2H_5OH, present in alcoholic drinks

antibiotic drug which destroys bacteria and so cures bacterial diseases

antiseptic chemical which kills bacteria in the environment

aqueous humour liquid found in the front part of the eyeball

asymmetrical having sides which do not match

atom smallest particle of an element

baccalauréat French school-leaving certificate

carbolic acid an early antiseptic used by Lister

crystal solid in which the atoms are arranged in a regular pattern; crystals of the same substance always have the same basic shape

dengue tropical disease caused by a virus and spread by mosquitoes

diphtheria bacterial disease which affects the throat

faculty group of departments in a university

fermentation process by which sugar is broken down into ethanol and carbon dioxide by the action of yeast in low levels of oxygen

French Revolution (1789–1799) very violent time in France when people fought for reforms and the monarchy ended

genetically engineered made by artificially changing DNA, or genes

guillotine device for cutting people's heads off, widely used in the French Revolution

hepatitis B very unpleasant disease of the liver

immune protected or safe from a disease

incubation period time between exposure to an infectious agent and the appearance of the symptoms of disease

infectious diseases diseases which are caused by an infectious agent such as a bacterium or a virus and which can be passed from one person to another

isomers two or more substances that are composed of the same elements in the same proportions but which have different properties because of differences in the arrangements of the atoms

leather tanners people who preserve or 'cure' animal skins to make them into flexible leather

malaria tropical disease of the blood spread by mosquitoes

militia group of armed people working for a particular leader or cause

molecule very small unit of a particular substance, made up of more than one atom joined together

Nobel prize awarded by the Nobel Foundation in memory of the Swedish scientist and inventor Alfred Nobel for outstanding achievement in physics, chemistry, medicine, literature, economics and for the promotion of world peace

optically active has an effect on polarized light

pasteurization method of reducing the number of micro-organisms present in liquids, such as milk, by heating, but not boiling

pébrine means 'pepper' – the name given to the silkworm disease which ravaged France and other silk-producing countries, so called because of the tiny brown or black spots which appeared on the animals

polarized light light in which the rays all travel in one direction

septicaemia blood poisoning, caused by bacteria

Shigella bacterium type of bacterium which causes dysentery – an infection of the bowel

spontaneous generation belief that living organisms could appear from nothing as a result of divine influence

spore the 'seed' of fungi and bacteria

stereochemistry study of the arrangement of atoms and molecules in space

sterile free from micro-organisms

tartrate a salt of tartaric acid, which is found in plants and fruit

vaccination method of innoculating someone with a strain of an infectious disease so that their immune system is prepared if and when they meet the live organism, and they do not suffer from the disease

vaccine weakened or dead strain of an infectious disease

Index